CHACE'S REVIVAL
BRAIN TUMOR & MULTIPLE STROKE SURVIVOR

CHACE GROVES

Contents

'

Chapter 1- Stuck and Waiting

I lie here in this dark room, wondering what time it is. It's been hours since my diaper was last changed. I opened my eyes about twenty minutes ago. I keep debating whether to press the call button. My left calf burns with pain, but I hate the idea of waking anyone up. Maybe if I could just straighten my leg out, it would help. The problem is, my legs don't fully work anymore. I've tried to push them, but they barely move. My right leg could use adjusting too, though it doesn't hurt nearly as much as the left. They shift around while I'm asleep — nerves and muscle spasms are to blame. That didn't start happening until this year.

Right now, both of my knees are twisted outward like I'm sitting Indian style. But I'm not sitting — I'm lying on my back in bed. I can't use my arms either. My dominant arm and hand are mostly paralyzed and barely responsive. My right arm still works, but just barely, and only within a limited range of motion.

I'm done trying to push my legs out. It's no use — they're not moving. I need to locate my call button. It's on a lanyard around my neck. I just need to grab the lanyard and feel my way down to the button. It's usually tucked under one of my armpits. The challenge is actually pressing it. I'm extremely weak — fingers, hands, arms, legs. Feet and toes too, I suppose. It just sounds silly listing them all.

Okay. There's the damn call button, jammed under my right armpit. It takes a few seconds to find the actual button buried beneath the red fabric that only looks like the button. I have to feel for it. My fingers are curled and rigid. I can't even pick my nose anymore.

I finally activate the button, but I can't hear the chime. I'm deaf in my left ear and can barely hear from my right. Still, I have to hope it worked. Now I wait.

Maybe fifteen minutes pass. My bedroom door creaks open, and my grandmother walks in. She approaches my bed as I ready myself to speak — swallowing saliva, inhaling air, mentally lining up words.
"What do you need?" she asks.
I try to say what's on the tip of my tongue. It should be so simple.

"Ey nee a my."

Damn it. Ran out of breath. She just stands there, staring at me, while I wait for my lungs to refill.

I inhale, exhale, repeat — trying to summon enough air to speak while she waits. This is so annoying. I can't talk well either. Sometimes my speech is decent, but that usually happens during the day — after I've had time to warm up. This difficulty is new too.

Oh, goody gumdrops. Here it comes. I inhale slowly, deeply, hoping to blurt something out in the process — no idea why. It never works.
"Mil egg hur."

Okay. Ready again.
"Straighten my ligs, plese."

She takes her time, carefully digging through the blankets like my legs are made of glass. One at a time.

My dad walks in. He looks half-asleep and annoyed. Without a word, he takes over — already knowing what's wrong. My grandmother slowly leaves the room. She is off the hook for now. My dad straightens my legs, gives them both a quick calf massage, and tucks the covers back in. He flashes the diver's "okay?" signal. I nod. His eyes are still barely open.

I feel bad for waking them, but I don't have many choices. I already tried waiting it out. But this isn't an itch. Pain doesn't fade just because you ignore it.

He's almost to the door.
"Wha tim is it?"

He glances at the clock, then holds up three fingers. He keeps walking. I roll my eyes. Only seven more hours. I fall back asleep.

I wake again. Open my eyes. Wonder what time it is now. The alarm clock is on the desk to my left. I try to lift my head high enough to read the digits on the digital screen. Of course, the alarm isn't set — I wouldn't be able to turn it off anyway. It's just there to check the time.

Problem is, I can't see it while lying flat. So here I am, attempting a massive crunch — even though most of my body's paralyzed. My core's getting stronger, but the first two attempts go nowhere. Not even close.

One last try. Deep breath. I tense my abs — push, push, push! I exhale hard and drop my head back.

No luck. I didn't hold the position long enough to focus. But I saw the middle number.
A two.

How much longer until my caregiver gets here? I need a good reason to push the call button for the second time this morning. I could use a drink, but that doesn't feel like a good enough excuse. I really wish I knew what time it was. Is anyone even up? I don't want to wake anyone again. I'll just lie here a while longer.

What do I want for breakfast? Cream of Wheat or pureed pancakes? What day is it? Oh — Friday. Shower day. That makes the decision easier. Cream of Wheat it is. It doesn't need to be blended, and I eat it faster. I still have swallowing issues and follow a pureed and thickened liquids diet. At least my feeding tube is gone. I hated that thing. I've still got a belly button-shaped dent on my stomach where it punctured the skin.

I've got lots of scars. Two on my head. One on my neck. One on each wrist. One on my right index finger.

My eyes shoot toward the bedroom door as it slowly opens, letting light spill into the room. Is it my caregiver? I hope so.

But no — can't be. She always flips the hallway light on first before coming in. I already know it's not her.

Here comes my grandma, carrying a plastic bag and a scooper for the litter box. She walks in, around the front of the TV, and through the double doors into the bathroom. My cat shoots out from under my bed, racing ahead to lead the way.

Several minutes later, she comes back through the double doors, smiling. I wait until she's close enough to hear me. I open my mouth, ready to speak — but nothing comes out. She walks around the front of the TV again and heads for the door. I swallow saliva and try to push out any sound at all. The bedroom door clicks shut behind her.

She's gone.

My cat's still in the bathroom. Still waiting for a treat, I guess. He doesn't understand that she's not coming back. His name's Jack, by the way. He likes pancakes. Just like me.

I'm lying here waiting for help, but I get distracted by the four recessed lights and the single smoke detector on the ceiling. I've played this game before.

The ceiling fan sits in the center — five blades, five gaps between them. I picture the recessed lights and the smoke detector sliding into the gaps between the blades, like puzzle pieces pulled into place. I feel this odd sense of satisfaction as they all slide back to their original positions.

I do it again. And again. Why? I don't know.

I'm interrupted. Maybe it's my caregiver?

Nope — it's my dad with my morning meds.

"Hurry up, I've got to get to work," he says. I don't sleep with my hearing aid in, so I can't hear him. Luckily, I'm decent at reading lips.

He sticks a wooden stick in my mouth while I'm trying to talk. My medicine's crushed and mixed with pudding. Still tastes awful. He turns to leave.

"Hey, was time es et?"

That came out pretty good. I smile at myself — but not for long.

"What!?" he says, turning back around.

I hate repeating myself. It already takes too much effort to say it once.

"What timb izzit?"

"Seven thirty," he says, and rushes out of the room.

Two and a half more hours. Time to connect dots on the ceiling, I guess.

Chapter 2- Another Day

What happened? I was sleeping so well, dreaming I was standing in the ocean, waves crashing gently against my back. I felt so happy. Then it just ended — and now I'm awake. Reality.

It must be getting close to time now, I think to myself. What do I want for breakfast? I start scrolling through the menu in my head. Then I remember — I already chose cream of wheat since it's a shower day.

I smile inwardly. I can't wait for my caregiver to wash my hair and scrub my scalp. My head itches, and it's so hard for me to reach. Most days, it goes unrelieved.

Then my bedroom lights come on. I know instantly who it is. I'm excited.

I made it, I like to think. I'm saved.

It's attention time. It feels so good when my caregiver walks in.

The door opens. Rachel walks in, waving. "Morning," she says as she heads to the desk to drop off her purse and hang up her coat. She knows my speech is usually poor in the mornings, so I just smile back instead of trying to respond.

She walks over, grabs my hearing aid, turns it on, and inserts it into my good ear.

"Can you hear me?" she asks. I nod.

It feels so good to hear again — like I'm finally on somewhat of a fair playing field.

She heads into the bathroom to gather supplies. The sound of the shower turning on echoes back as she returns with clean clothes, fresh bed sheets, a few towels, and my lift sling.

She starts to remove my diaper, but I stop her.
"Let me pee one more time," I say.
She giggles and says okay.

I stare at the wall and imagine I'm underground in a sewer, running through shallow water as it splashes everywhere. I picture myself carrying a pipe wrench, tightening leaks as water pours in from both an overhead pipe and some kind of spillway gate.

"Okay," I tell Rachel, signaling that it's probably safe to remove the diaper. I've been wrong before. I just can't feel it the way I used to. It's strange — sometimes I can pee easily, other times I have to really push. And I can't hold it in anymore. Don't ask me how that works. Ready or not, here it comes.

She rolls me across the bed onto my right side and removes my ever-so-glamorous, urine-soaked diaper. She places the rolled-up sling under where my back had been lying. Then she rolls me onto my left side to unroll the other half. Now the sling is laid out flat beneath me.

She connects the sling's four corner straps to the lift and grabs the controller.
With the push of a button, I slowly rise — like a nude angel ascending into the sky.

My shower chair is already waiting. As she wheels me over, I imagine I look like a trapped pig in a net, hanging from a tree. She lowers me into the chair and unhooks the straps.

We head into the bathroom. The shower chair is basically an unpadded wheelchair.
She parks me against the vanity and holds me up so I don't fall. Then, she begins brushing my teeth. I'll admit — it tickles — but I try to keep it together.

I rinse and spit a few times. She cleans everything up, removes my hearing aid, and I can no longer hear the shower water running.

We roll straight into the shower. There's no door — it's like a drive-in car wash for me and my chair.

She parks me and sprays water all over my body so I can test the temperature. We have to be careful — I hate getting burnt. I nod my approval, and here we go.

Scrub-a-dub-dub.

My hair, mustache, and beard are scrubbed clean — now food-free.

She does an amazing job. I'm as clean as a cat that slipped and fell into a bathtub. But it's not as simple as it sounds.

Rachel has to hold me upright the entire time — I tend to lean right and could easily fall. She constantly watches me to make sure I don't slide out of the chair. She even has to lean me forward to wash my back.

It feels good having my feet on the ground, but she's got to grab me just right, or I'll spill out like dirt dumped from a wheelbarrow.

We roll out of the shower and towel off. She tilts the chair back and heads to my bed to change the sheets. Once that's done, she returns and reattaches the straps of the sling to the lift. I always double-check the straps—just for peace of mind, not because I don't trust her. I just need to know I'm secure and won't end up on the floor.

She lifts me back up and lowers me gently onto the bed. She dries me a bit more, then puts on a clean diaper—which I instantly pee in without saying anything. Once I'm dressed, she props me up in bed and adjusts everything without being asked. She makes sure I'm comfortable, then brushes my hair and beard.

"What do you want to eat?" she asks.

I try to say, "Cream of Wheat and yogurt." It doesn't come out perfectly, but she nods to show she understood.

"And chocolate milk."

She nods again, then hands me my phone and call button before stepping out to prepare breakfast.

I check email and scroll through social media while I wait. My phone is mounted on a stand because I can't hold it, and I use a stylus to operate it—my fingers are curled and clumsy. It took a lot of practice and effort to get to this point.

It's such a relief to have help from someone who notices even the smallest discomforts. Sometimes when she's not here, I feel off, but can't explain why. That's incredibly frustrating. Communication isn't easy.

Rachel returns with breakfast—food in one hand, drink in the other. She sets everything on my bed tray and grabs a bib. Then she places a red foam cylinder in my right hand. It's hollow in the middle, and she slips the spoon handle inside. That gives me something big enough to grip, even when my hand is weak.

She bibs me up, and I begin feeding myself like a toddler—dropping food in my beard all over again. It's messy, but I'm doing it. While I eat, she takes my vitals, then wipes me down.

I just peed again, but I don't say anything. I'm not ready to be changed yet.

I finish breakfast without trouble. I usually cough and sometimes choke, but not today. I've improved, but when choking gets bad, I start to zone out. The room fades, my hearing dulls, my body tingles. It takes time to come back from that. Thankfully, it doesn't happen as often anymore.

Now for the fun part. Rachel brings a small cup of crushed pills mixed with pudding. She starts to spoon-feed me.

"No medicine today—it's my birthday," I joke. The words come out fairly clear.

She doesn't laugh. I've used that excuse way too many times.

I take the mud-like mix, plus two more scoops. Then I finish my drink.

"What shake do you want for lunch?" she asks.

"Chocolate. Life's too short for vanilla."

She smiles and heads to the kitchen. She always makes the shake ahead of time and puts it in the fridge.

She returns shortly. We don't have much time left. I'm ready for my afternoon nap. She uses the bed remote to lay me flat, then grabs supplies for a quick change before lunch. She swaps out the pee pad. Apparently, I soaked it pretty well.

I'm exhausted. Showers wear me out. Good thing they're only twice a week. Neither of us could handle more. She wipes me down daily, so I'm not stinking up the place—but full showers are only on Tuesdays and Thursdays.

Rachel raises the bed again so I can drink my shake. It's a little thick because she adds thickener to make it safer for me to swallow. I actually like these shakes.

She props me upright, makes a few posture adjustments, and starts to feed me the shake.

I take a few gulps, pause to breathe, take a few more. Then I stop. There's a tickle in my nose.

Uh oh. I lose control of my face. My eyes flutter open and shut. My body jerks backward against the bed. I suck in air through my nose. Once. Twice. Again and again. It probably looks like I'm having a seizure. One inhale per jerk. Then, just like that, it stops.

Rachel watches closely—she knows by now this is just my body trying to sneeze. It never finishes. Why? I don't know. Just another mystery in this mess. She helps me blow my nose. I finish the shake.

As I drink, my mind drifts again. How did I end up like this? Why me? What did I do to deserve this?

I try to stop the thoughts. Focus on swallowing.

I finish my shake. Rachel cleans up and takes the trash. When she comes back, she makes sure I'm comfortable. Then she grabs her things.

"Bye," she says.

"Thank you," I try to say.

She smiles and gives me a thumbs-up.

The door shuts. I'm left with my thoughts. Lying there. Tired. Upset. Remembering the past.

Chapter 3 – The Tainted Seed

I'm tired. I find myself thinking back to how all of this began. I actually remember quite a lot—probably more than people expect, considering the circumstances. It all started thirty-four years ago. I had just completed my nine-month transformation in the womb, and the next chapter of my life had begun. The year was 1987. December 15th. Bedford, Texas. That's where I exited my human portal. I'm not sure anyone realized that this life would be anything but normal . From the beginning, this seed was planted with struggle.

At first, everything seemed fine. I was your average adorable baby. It was just my mother, father, sister, and me. My sister had a six-year head start. A few years later, my parents built a house in a small Texas town, and that's when my brother arrived.

I attended a local Mother's Day Out program and kept getting sick. My parents were notified, and a doctor ordered that unforgettable first MRI. Of course, I had no idea what was happening—I was only four years old. I didn't understand that the giant tunnel-like machine was taking pictures of my brain, or that those images would explain why my life wouldn't follow the path of a fairytale with a happy ending.

While I was inside that machine, vital information was being revealed—and soon, the answer would come. That's when my parents were told something no one wants to hear: there was something wrong with my brain. I think about how hard that moment must have been for them, and for my sister too. I was only a toddler.

My parents were informed that I had a tumor growing on my brain. The even more serious problem? It was on my brain stem. I don't remember any of this, but I've been told the story many times.

I'm still here, right where my caregiver left me. I'm propped up just enough to see the clock with some effort. It's only four. My mouth is dry. I need a drink—then I might be able to go to sleep. I feel around for the call button and press it.

Or… did I just think about pressing it?

That happens a lot. I second-guess myself and consider pressing it again, just to be sure. But I hesitate. I don't want to get in trouble for pushing it twice. So, I decide to wait and see what happens. Ten minutes—or what feels like ten minutes—pass. I finally decide to press it again… or maybe for the first time? My memory fails me.

I feel around, locate the call button again, and search for the actual press point. Before I can push it, my door opens.

Guess I did press it the first time.

I was a heartbeat away from pressing it again. My short-term memory is a mess.

My grandma walks in and asks what I need. I try to tell her I need water, but the words don't come. I shake my head and open and close my mouth like a dog trying to catch air. It only lasts a few seconds. Then I take a breath and try again.

"Wadder," I say.

"You need some water?" she asks. I nod yes.

She raises the upper part of my bed and holds my head up. Then she grabs a cup from my overbed table and brings it to my lips. I drink the small amount of water in two gulps.

"More," I say.

She takes the cup to the kitchen to refill it and add the thickener I need. I close my eyes and wait. My mind drifts back to the tumor—what I actually remember.

I remember arriving at the hospital. My maternal grandfather was waiting under the covered entrance as we pulled up. Later, I remember being strapped to a table in a big, dark room.

Before I can drift off again, Grandma returns with more water. She gives me a few gulps. I'm refreshed. I give her a thumbs-up to let her know I'm good. She puts the cup back and leaves.

Back to the memories…

I was only four, so maybe some of them are exaggerated. Still, I remember arriving at the hospital again—maybe a different day. I was in a dark room with my dad and a technician. I was holding a duck stuffed animal and biting my dad's finger while they tried to give me a shot. I kept squirming and was told I broke the needle. The technician strapped me down and tried again. I wasn't very happy with her after that.

I remember being taken outside a few times to play. Nurses brought me popsicles. My sister gave me a stuffed bear. I remember a lobby-like area where my aunt and I drew and colored together. I remember waking up in the middle of the night, hearing people outside my door. I looked at my dad—he was asleep in a chair beside me. I stared out the dark window in my door, trembling in fear, hoping no one would come in.

The plan was to terminate the tumor with radiation and remove it through the back of my neck. I had multiple rounds of radiation each day, focused on the sides of my head. That's why I don't grow hair around my ears anymore. And now I have a long scar running down the back of my neck. My balance, speech, hearing, and coordination all suffered in the process.

After the hospital, I was moved into a crib in my parents' room. A toy hammock filled with stuffed animals hung above me. I was placed on a home-based speech and language program. My hearing and balance were decent—but not good enough to walk a tightrope or hear a mouse sneeze. For the next several years, I had an MRI and a check-up every year at the hospital.

My childhood was pretty good. My parents took my brother and me on many trips—to the ocean and on ski vacations. We weren't spoiled, but we never went without. When I started school, I was placed in an assisted learning program as well as a special reading class. I didn't attend the regular reading class with the other kids. Though I could hear just fine, the school hearing test revealed some weaknesses. I joined the Boy Scouts of America and loved it. I also played little league baseball.

Middle school went okay. I eventually started attending regular reading classes. Eventually, other kids began noticing my scar and the bald patches around my ears from surgery. They teased me relentlessly—not just because of my appearance, but also because I was very short. I hadn't even realized these things about myself until others pointed them out. I began to hate school.

Around that time, my sister graduated and moved out, which brought my brother and me even closer. We spent our days swimming in the backyard pool and playing rollerblade hockey in the driveway with the neighborhood kids. I also developed a deep love for building bricks. My circle of friends mostly came from my Boy Scout troop. I suppose you could say I was shy and not very good at making friends outside of that. I didn't play school sports because I was terrified of messing up in front of everyone. I had a very low self-esteem, but I was thriving in Scouts. I belonged to a very active troop and handled camping, hiking, and all the activities just fine.

We moved to an even smaller town when I started high school. Despite the long commute, I stayed in my Boy Scout troop. In school, I made a few friends through our shared interest in cars. I earned my Eagle Scout rank in 2003 and graduated in 2006 in a class of about twenty students. That same year, my oldest nephew—my sister's first child—was born.

My love for building bricks gradually turned into an interest in design. I spent hours every day drawing houses and buildings, both by hand and on the computer. After high school, I moved back to my hometown and lived with my sister. I worked for a commercial painting company and started college. My brother graduated high school in 2010, the same year my sister gave birth to my first niece.

I rescued Jack as a kitten. After switching jobs and exploring different industries, I finally earned my associate's degree in 2012—the year my second niece was born. By then, I had moved several times and lived in different apartments. My interest in design had grown into a serious passion. Drawing floor plans became my greatest hobby, taking up nearly all my free time.

I decided to pursue my dream of becoming an architect. I enrolled in a local university's architecture program.

That's when my life took a drastic turn.

Chapter 4- Red Flags

I just woke up from a very good nap. I crashed hard. It's dinnertime, and I'm soaked in urine. I desperately need to be changed. My body is twisted into an uncomfortable shape. My head isn't even on the pillow anymore.

I grope around for the call button and press it. Now I wait, staring up at the ceiling.

I begin to wonder if the crown molding could slide over to one side and align with the other. I'm not sure why this thought returns—what's stranger is that I've already solved this, several times. The ceiling drops down in a stepped design, so the second tier of molding is an offset copy of the first. I'd estimate the offset at about sixteen inches.

The room is rectangular, with a short hallway leading to the door. In my mind, I draw tick marks on the two long sides of the first tier to show they're equal. Then I add double tick marks on the top and bottom—also equal, but different from the sides.

Now I imagine the bottom piece of the second tier sliding left until it touches the wall. I'm trying to prove that the once-overhanging molding, in front of the jogged section that serves as the hallway, won't match the length of the first-tier molding, which is cut short to make space for the same hallway.

My grandma pops in. Despite my body being zigzagged all over the place, she still asks what I need. Not ready to speak, I say, "My legs," fairly clearly. I hope she'll figure it out.

She uncovers my legs and tries to straighten them, one at a time. I try to help. Sometimes I can push just a little—it doesn't always work well, and sometimes not at all. I clench my fists and push hard. My face twists into something between furious and constipated. I concentrate, trying to move my hip. The right side shifts slightly, causing my leg to loosen and straighten while she's still working on the left one. I fart during the process. All is well.

I try to wiggle myself back into position. I push so hard I feel like I'm going to pop a blood vessel in my forehead. My upper body starts to shift into place. Then suddenly, my body jerks. My fists shoot up and start shaking uncontrollably. My right leg snaps up into the shape of a gabled roof. My head shakes involuntarily, and I'm making low, grunting sounds. I hate this part. Some kind of nerve thing— it's like my limbs are resisting. My hands are still bouncing like I'm shaking imaginary maracas, but eventually everything else stops. They're slowing down. Just a few more seconds.

My grandma asks if I'm okay. I push again. Both of my legs slowly straighten out and lie flat. My body is straight now—but I'm too far down in bed.

Already knowing what she'll say, I tell her anyway: "I'm too low in bed."

"I can't pull you up!" she says.

"I know," I reply.

She asks if I want to sit up to eat. I remind her I can't sit up—or eat—until I'm repositioned. "You'll have to wait for your dad to get home from work," she says, stating the obvious.

Usually I get changed before eating, so I'm not laid back down with food still settling. That's caused problems before. I realize I'm extremely thirsty, but I can't have a drink either. Swallowing's hard enough when I'm sitting up. I aspirate and choke. I spend most of the day clearing my throat between meals.

Once she leaves the room, I return to trying to remember what happened after I earned my associate's degree. I had gone to university to pursue a degree in architecture—but something happened.

Oh, right. I remember now.

Around that time, my hearing became much worse. My ears were ringing constantly. I had been losing hearing gradually over the years, but this was a big drop. I don't know when I went deaf in my left ear. I bought a hearing aid for my right ear, which helped a lot.

Classes began, but I still had trouble understanding my professors. After talking with some staff, I was able to rent a hearing device from campus. It was a microphone that clipped to the professor's clothes and sent their voice directly to my hearing aid. It worked well in the larger classrooms.

One day, when I wasn't in school, I was running errands with my oldest nephew in the back seat. It had been a productive day. We were heading back to my sister's house when I drove through a short tunnel. My window was down, so I didn't think much when I heard a popping sound—I figured I ran over a chip bag or something. A few seconds later, my vision got blurry and started shaking side to side. I didn't know what was happening.

I spotted an empty parking lot on the left. I planned to turn in and call for help. I waited for traffic to clear, blinker on. I could still see the cars well enough and felt safe to turn—but I didn't want to risk it with my nephew in the truck.

I got his attention and asked him to tell me when it was safe. He was eager to help. When we both agreed it was clear, I turned into the lot and parked. I rolled down the windows and opened the sunroof, Turned off the ignition, and put the keys in the cupholder.

I took a few minutes to think. I explained to my nephew what was happening. My vision started clearing, but I was scared it might come back. I made some calls, including to my doctor. No one had answers. We eventually made it home safely.

A few days later, at work—back when I was a cashier—it happened again. Over the course of an hour, my vision got so blurry I could barely see a few feet ahead. It was almost lunchtime, so I took an early break. After resting, I felt better. I suspected it was a major eye strain.

Not long after that, my hearing worsened again. I could tell the issue wasn't my hearing aid—it was my ear. My sister helped me find an ENT that didn't require insurance. We booked the earliest appointment we could.

At the Ear, Nose, and Throat doctor, I mentioned not only my hearing difficulties but also my earlier vision issues. After several unsuccessful attempts to sell me a new hearing aid, he paused and said he suspected I might have Meniere's disease. He recommended an MRI. That would be my first MRI since childhood.

A few weeks later, I had the MRI and returned to the ENT to get my results. During that visit, he pointed out that I had several spots of white matter on my brain. He said the spots were common with aging and that I shouldn't worry. My hearing returned a few days later.

About a month after that, I was sitting on campus after class, chatting with classmates. Suddenly, voices around me began to sound metallic—distorted and unnatural. Alarmed, I excused myself and went to the restroom. Standing at the vanity, I looked at myself in the mirror and removed my hearing aid. I was deeply concerned. I splashed cold water on my face and ears, then put the aid back in. The distortion remained.

I walked out and immediately called my ENT, my hearing aid specialist, and my primary care physician. It was after hours. All the offices were closed. I felt helpless.

Since then, my hearing has come and gone. Sometimes it disappears at night, sometimes gradually during the day. When it goes, it usually returns within days—but occasionally, it takes up to two weeks.

At the same time, I was struggling to focus. I brought my concerns to staff members and eventually made the painful decision to give up my dream of becoming an architect. I left the university, prematurely, without a degree. That same year, my brother gave me my third niece. She was born prematurely.

But I wasn't done with school—not yet. I moved in with my dad and stopped working. I enrolled in a vocational college. I still wanted to learn the

computer-aided design software I hadn't had the
chance to study at the university.

My dad walks into my room. I snap out of sleep.
He changes my diaper, lays down a clean pee pad,
and pulls me up in bed. He looks tired.

He sets my phone and its stand in front of me and
asks if I've eaten. I say I've been waiting to be
pulled up. He says dinner will be ready in an hour.

I glance at my phone. It's almost 8 p.m. I check
my email and scroll through social media while I
wait. After Dad helps me eat, I take my medicine.
Then we brush my teeth. And he lays me back
down for bed.

I fall asleep instantly.

Chapter 5- Man Down

I wake up, and from the sunlight streaming through the gaps in the blinds, it seems late in the morning. I hit the call button to let everyone know I'm awake, then begin wiping the sleep from my eyes with my right hand. My mind starts flipping through breakfast options like a mental menu.

Then I remember—it's Saturday, and Rachel isn't working today. I'm still waiting on someone to come. I stare at the ceiling. I notice a few imperfections. The painter clearly didn't spend nearly as much time inspecting the ceiling as I am now.

Thinking back on my situation, I try to remember what came next.

After leaving architecture school, I moved in with my dad. I stored all my belongings and enrolled in a vocational college just five minutes away. I took a machining class and several courses in computer-aided design and building information modeling. I loved it. I was having so much fun working with milling machines, lathes, 3D printers, a laser cutter, and a variety of design software.

Before I even finished school, I landed a job in the industry. I worked three days a week, balancing it with my classes, and for the first time in a long while, I had weekends off. I loved the job even more than school. Everything was going great. I was finally about to graduate and move on to the next stage of my life. After ten years of college—traditional classes, weekend classes, summer classes, mini-semesters, night courses, and online courses—I was proud, relieved, and ready.

The door finally cracks open, snapping me out of my thoughts. I try to remember what I need. It's my grandma again. She comes over to my bedside and asks what I need. I rub my belly in slow, clockwise circles and tell her I'm hungry. I was hoping the motion would help clarify what I meant, but she asks if my stomach hurts. I roll my eyes, frustrated, trying to hold back. I yell out, "I'M HUNGRY!"

"Oh! What would you like to eat?" she asks.

"Pancake," I reply.

She turns slowly and walks out. It'll take a while.

My mind drifts again. I remember being just two weeks away from graduation, alternating workdays with school. Life was good. Everything felt perfect.

It was April 2016. I woke up one morning and went to work like usual. On the drive, I noticed something strange—my leg felt weak. I felt off.

I arrived at work and it persisted throughout the day. I eventually asked my coworkers what they thought, and my boss told me to head home after lunch and rest.

I decided to go to the hospital. My mother was in town, so I called her and asked if she could take me.

Once I got home, I remembered—I didn't have medical insurance. My mother suggested I take a nap and see how I felt afterward. I was exhausted, so I agreed.

But when I woke up, it was worse. My leg was dragging, and I was limping. My mother agreed we should go to the hospital. She drove me and dropped me off at the emergency room. I remember hobbling in and that I was the only patient in the waiting room. The front desk gave me a clipboard and told me to have a seat. I was shocked. Really? I could barely walk. I took the clipboard and made my way to the closest chair.

I struggled to write legibly. I was halfway through the first page when my mother came in from parking the car. She must've said something, because the chatty girls at the front desk suddenly went quiet. One of them quickly stood up and escorted me to an exam room. My mother followed.

I remember the hallway—the chair molding along the wall—and how my left shoulder had slumped down to that height. It felt like the entire left side of my body was melting.

We waited a while before a doctor came in. He ran a few basic tests—smile, raise your arms, follow my finger, touch my nose—standard stuff. Then he left. The next wait felt endless. Hours later, another doctor came in, repeated a few of the same tests, and ordered an MRI. When the results came back, they said it looked normal. They discharged me that evening.

I worked from home for the next few weeks. I used a rollator to get around because my left leg was dragging like dead weight. We still had no idea what was happening. My parents and I went from doctor to doctor looking for answers.

Then, one day, the burning started. My left leg felt like they the calf was on fire. My sister took off work and drove me to a larger hospital. After hours of waiting, they drew blood and reviewed my previous MRI. I was sent home again. Still no answers. I felt completely hopeless.

In the days that followed, I started experiencing intense pain whenever I sneezed. It felt like being whipped—lightning-bolt-shaped, scattered, and vicious. Every time I sneezed, I dropped to the ground, screaming, rolling my back across the carpet, desperate for any kind of relief. The pain only lasted a few seconds, but it felt like forever.

Graduation finally arrived, and I walked the stage for the last time with a certificate in Drafting and Design. I no longer needed my rollator. I walked with a bit of a wobble, and I probably looked like a penguin in my black gown. My tassel swung wildly, like a wind chime in a storm. I made it. I was done with school at last. Later that year, my second nephew was born.

My family found a specialist doctor, and we decided to seek help from him and his team. I released all of my MRIs and medical records. That's when I received the phone call that changed everything.

A few days later, while I was at work, I got a call from the specialist team. They informed me that I had suffered a stroke and needed to check into another hospital for a couple of weeks. I trembled. I had expected this news, but hearing it from a specialist made it feel real. I was shaking so badly I could barely use my computer mouse and keyboard. I told my boss, and he let me go—encouraging me to focus on my health.

I checked into the hospital preferred by the specialist. The team was ready for me. They told me that the MRI previously ordered by the ENT actually showed strokes. My mind raced. Had we known that earlier—could all this have been avoided? Why didn't anyone tell me? Why had I been told not to worry? Were my shaking eyes and hearing changes symptoms of the stroke?

During my stay, I underwent more MRIs, a CT scan, an EKG, and a lumbar puncture. I was diagnosed with foot drop and fitted with a brace for my left foot. I also received some physical and occupational therapy. Then came the news I feared most—but expected.

Instead of moving into my own apartment and moving forward with my career, my mother told me I'd be moving in with her so she could care for me during the day. It was the opposite of what I wanted.

My parents didn't live together. She lived at the lakefront property where I had stayed during high school. I didn't want to live with anyone. I wanted independence. I wasn't ready to accept this new reality.

I was devastated—angry, depressed, and heartbroken. I felt like my life was unraveling. I remember being at my dad's office one day. I walked out into the middle of the street and lay down. I wanted it to be over. I felt cheated. I closed my eyes. I heard several cars drive around me. After a while, the noise stopped and I felt that someone was watching me.

I opened my eyes to see a car stopped still in front of me. I stood up to let it pass. But the car didn't move. I looked through the windshield—and realized the driver was my occupational therapist. I had forgotten she was scheduled to visit that day.

Grandma brought in my breakfast and left. Pancakes are one of the meals I can eat without help. I try to be as independent as I can, whenever I can. Jack jumps up on the bed and watches me eat.

Chapter 6- A New Beginning

Grandma comes back in and clears away the breakfast dishes. She helps me finish off my drink, then quietly leaves the room. I manage to grab the bed remote and lower myself down. I probably lowered myself too far after eating, but my left leg is cramping.

It had already started hurting before I ate, but I didn't say anything—I needed to eat first before anyone could do something about it. I often keep things to myself. Over time, I've grown more tolerant of pain. I can ignore it for quite a while now. That doesn't mean I'm immune to it.

So I'm lying here. Weekends feel slow and uneventful without Rachel. I usually don't get much attention. I just rest and think. My mind starts to drift again.

We're on our way to the house. I used to visit it during summer breaks when I was in college, but I hadn't lived there since high school.

We pull into the driveway, and my mother gets out to open the gate. She returns, and we roll slowly down the awkwardly steep path. The road sits about twenty feet above the house's foundation and drops sharply. The driveway curves slightly too—like a giant slide.

We unloaded the car, and I took my rollator down by the water. I just sat and watched—the lake, the sunset, the hills. Everything felt still.

Over the next several days, Jack explored the great outdoors and made himself right at home. He quickly figured out the doggy door and came and went as he pleased. My mother had two small dogs and two large ones. They were fenced in with gates and pens, but Jack jumped over them and roamed free. He made friends with a couple of feral cats. He explored by day and curled up in bed with me by night.

I found so much joy in watching the young perch swim in the shallow water under my great-grandfather's old metal jon boat. It rested just above the lake on a trolley under a roof. I began feeding the fish breadcrumbs, pickles, and slices of banana. More and more came. I loved watching them race toward the food.

Soon, I wanted to see them more closely. I placed a net on the bottom of the shallow water, which was only about a foot deep. I hid my shadow by peeking over the edge of the boat and pulled up the net when the fish swam over it. I got such a thrill out of it. I loved admiring the different colors of the baby fish and identifying their types. I always returned them to the water—I just liked looking.

It wasn't long before I became interested in the bigger fish. I tossed handfuls of cat food into the deeper water and watched as fish swarmed it like piranhas. On our next trip into town, I bought a fishing license, a rod, and a tackle box. I began catching perch, catfish, bass, crappie, and carp. I was having a blast.

Fishing became more than a hobby—it was helping me regain what I had lost from the stroke. The hours spent casting, reeling, walking, pulling, and tying knots were therapy. But I wasn't done. I wanted to go out further into the lake.

I didn't want to use a motorboat—I wanted a kayak. My dad bought me a sit-on-top kayak, and we tried it out. I could barely sit on it without tipping over whenever a wave came by. I was too weak to balance. My dad gave me some tough love. He told me I wouldn't be able to ride it on my own. We practiced re-entering the kayak after falling off. I did terribly. I swallowed so much lake water.

The next day, I made it my number one goal: I was going to get on and stay on that kayak by myself. Nearly every day, I got out there. I started paddling while the kayak was tied to the dock. I began doing water aerobics—kicking while holding the dock, wading through the water, stretching my arms. I flipped the kayak on purpose and practiced climbing back on. I even worked on turning and shifting around while sitting on it.

It was hard work, but I was determined to prove myself.

Before long, I was racing—dock to dock, forward and backward. I felt nearly as strong as I was before the stroke, except for a small limp. I began venturing farther across the lake, though I never went more than a mile from home. I brought my tackle box and poles with me, exploring and watching nature. I saw turtles, snakes, a sunken paddleboat, and even found a few snagged lures. I lost several of my own, too—snagged on rocks, weeds, even tree branches.

Eventually, I felt the urge to conquer the steep driveway on foot. I made it only a few yards before falling on my backside. I scooted back down, defeated but not discouraged. I added the climb to my daily routine. I fell often. My knees, elbows, and hands were constantly scraped. My mother told me not to go up there, which only made me want it more.

Coming down was the hardest part. Balancing against the pull of gravity was brutal. I was still dealing with foot drop. Adjusting my ankles at the right angle and applying pressure was difficult—especially with the foot brace. Still, I kept at it. I even bought a stationary bike to help me build strength.

I started driving myself, in my mother's car, to and from nearby stores. I often went places with my mother, and I was walking very well. I no longer needed my rollator.

I had recovered more than just well. I had conquered the stroke. Almost two years had gone by since I was hospitalized. I felt free. The stroke no longer defined me. I won, and was moving on.

Chapter 7- OFF GUARD

Here I was, thinking about how far I had come and how proud I was of myself. Things were okay. I made them okay. I worked hard. I made it. So where did things go wrong—and why? What was so wrong with staying where I was? If only things hadn't changed.

On Valentine's Day in 2018, I woke up to another stroke. I don't clearly remember how I felt that morning—just that something wasn't right. I told my mother to call 911. One of my first thoughts was whether the ambulance would even be able to make it down and then back up that steep driveway.

I knew I'd be going to the same hospital as before and wondered if I'd see any of the same people again.

My speech was slightly slurred. I think my arms, hands, and fingers were okay at that point. I knew the ambulance had arrived because my mother's dogs started barking. I was wheeled out on a stretcher and loaded into the van. They strapped me in, and we began the hour-long commute. As we started up the steep driveway, it felt like we barely made it to the top.

At the hospital, I did see my nurse aide from the last stroke. She was now working in the ER. The MRI technologist was the same as before, too.

I ended up staying in the hospital for a few days. MRIs, imaging, and other tests were done. I remember waking up with a massive migraine—three mornings in a row. They were horrible. I would sit on the bed backward, on my knees, banging my head against the wall. I remember a strong, clean scent in my nose. It burned, like snorting laundry detergent. It smelled vaguely like lavender.

Nothing the hospital gave me relieved the pain. It was awful. This stroke was similar to the first, except it affected the opposite side. Now I limped on both sides when walking. The doctor adjusted some of my home medications, and I was discharged.

That first night at home was a long one. I stayed up worrying, afraid I'd wake up with another migraine. When I finally woke the next morning without a migraine and without that awful burning in my nose, I was relieved.

I could still move almost everything, but I was very weak. Now, both sides of my body were "weaker." Still, I got back to fishing, kayaking, swimming, and exercising. It was tough being weak on both sides, but I was determined to get stronger—again.

My mother and I made many trips to doctors, trying to get answers. Why was I having these strokes? We were told they were caused by bleeding in the brain. Most doctors pointed to the brain tumor as the cause.

There wasn't full agreement on the specifics. Some doctors believed my artery walls had been weakened by radiation during tumor treatment, causing them to rupture. The bleeding restricted oxygen to parts of my brain.
Another theory was that scar tissue from the tumor caused inflammation and other complications. I'm no doctor, but I had my doubts.

A few months later, my maternal grandmother unexpectedly passed away. We moved into her house to take care of my mother's stepfather. I no longer lived by the lake. I continued physical therapy at our new address and made good progress.

My daily lake routine of fishing, swimming, and kayaking was replaced with other exercises—like walking up and down the long driveway with my rollator.

Once I regained some strength, I began driving myself to church, the gym, stores, and a nearby state park. I joined the gym to keep improving. Most days, I was the only one there, which I liked. My right arm was much stronger than my left. I kept the weights low—but heavy enough to get results. The last thing I needed was an injury. I lifted with both arms, but never at the same time. The difference between them was about fifteen pounds.

I also used a stationary bike, leg press, and did mat exercises. I was improving again and proving myself once more.

Christmas came, and I was excited to see family. On December 21, 2019, my brother was on his way to our house. But instead of seeing him, I was riding in an ambulance to a new hospital. An MRI confirmed yet another stroke

I stayed in the hospital for about a month and received physical, occupational, and speech therapy. A swallowing study showed I was having trouble with liquids, so I was put on thickened drinks. I hated that part—and I hated speech therapy—but I loved physical and occupational therapy. We worked hard and played hard in PT. I spent Christmas and New Year's in the hospital. It was quiet. All the good nurses and therapists were off. I was temporarily given a modified walker with an elevated rest for my left hand.

This time around, things were harder. Even though I'd worked hard in therapy, I was still struggling. Walking was a big challenge. I could only manage a few yards before needing a rest. I relied mostly on a power wheelchair. It was pretty fast. I remember driving at top speed around the patio furniture, like I was barrel racing. I also spent more time drawing houses on my computer, since I couldn't move as much.

I'm waiting on lunch, and my left leg hurts pretty badly. That probably means I've been ignoring it for too long. My mouth is very dry, too. Coincidentally, my dad walks in.

"You okay?" he asks.

I shake my head no. He closes the door behind him and steps closer.

"What do you need?"

"I need a drink," I tell him.

He grabs my cup from the bedside table. "And my leg hurts," I add, once I have enough breath again. I say it in that order because I want some water before he lays me down.

He leaves the room and returns with a fresh cup. Lifting my head gently, he holds the cup so I can drink. I gulp loudly—a dozen swallows or more. Then he sets the cup back down and rolls the table away from the bed.

He lowers the bed until it's flat, then pulls back the covers. My left leg is twisted at an angle, almost like I've been sitting cross-legged but lying down. It looks uncomfortable because it is. He pulls the pee pad beneath me toward himself, shifting my lower body back into alignment. Relief floods through me.

"Better?" he asks.

I nod.

He tucks the blanket around my legs again and asks, "What shake do you want?"

"Vanilla," I say, and he leaves the room.

I wish Rachel were here to stretch my arms and legs. I wish we could afford to have her a few more hours each week. I always feel better when she's around. When she leaves, I just wait anxiously for her next visit. I feel more human when she's here. My body feels more manageable. My life feels more manageable.

Dad returns with the shake. He raises the bed again and holds the cup while I drink. A few gulps at a time, then a breath. A few more gulps. When I finish, he wipes my mouth and rolls the table back in place so I can have my phone.

"Do we have time for the wheelchair today?" I ask.

"Not today," he says. "I've got a lot to do. Maybe tomorrow."

Only fifty-something hours until Rachel comes back, I think to myself, watching him walk out the door.

Chapter 8 - Derailed

I'm sitting here, bored out of my mind. My lungs aren't clear. I can feel my body trying to cough, but it's not as simple as it used to be. I want to cough, but I can't summon the strength in my chest to do it. I wish Rachel were here. She listens to my lungs with her stethoscope, turns me onto my side, and gently thumps on my back. I usually burp a few times, and that helps clear things out. But for now, I'll have to keep trying—sticking my tongue out like I'm gagging to trigger something.

I'm trying to think back. I used to walk, talk, swallow, eat, and use my right arm, hand, and fingers. I used a powered wheelchair, but mostly for going outside. I could walk to the toilet and take care of things on my own. I remember Christmas of 2020—I got to be home with my family. My aunt and brother brought their families over to visit. It felt good to spend the holidays at home and not in the hospital that year.

A couple of days later, on December 27th, I woke up with a headache and had trouble getting to the bathroom. My legs were very weak, and I kept falling. I yelled to my mother for help as I crawled around on the floor, searching for anything to help pull myself up. I was slurring my words, in a bad mood, and struggling to hear or understand her. I kept insisting I didn't need to go to the hospital, but despite what I said, she called 911. An ambulance came and took me to the same hospital as the year before.

I don't remember the ride or arriving. I only remember brief moments in the ER. I called my sister on speakerphone and could barely manage even do that. I set the phone down on the bed—I couldn't hold it in my hands. I don't know if she answered or not. I told her I couldn't hear her but just wanted her to know I was back in the hospital. I did the same for my dad. I remember a small blood stain on the bed sheets where they had spilled some while drawing blood. I also remember feeling excited when I was told I'd be moved upstairs."Will I have my own bathroom?"—a ridiculous question, considering I could barely move, let alone walk. I just knew I hated using a bedpan for the first time.

Dinner arrived, and I choked miserably on the water. I was confused and embarrassed, glancing around to make sure no one noticed. I was moved upstairs to a new room. By then, I was completely paralyzed.

Later, I was taken downstairs for a swallowing evaluation. I was sure I had passed with flying colors—but they said I had failed miserably. I was shocked. I had already missed lunch while being evaluated. Then the doctor told me I needed a feeding tube. I refused. I didn't want one. He told me I wouldn't be able to eat, drink, or take medicine without it. I refused again—and didn't get dinner.

That night dragged on. Not because I hadn't eaten, but because I couldn't turn my brain off. I didn't sleep at all. I didn't sleep the next night either—or the one after that. I lay there, wide awake, with my mind racing. I remember looking out the window at the parking garage across the street. I imagined taking a giant cookie cutter to the spaces between the concrete columns—just cutting out shapes, over and over.

After dozens of imaginary cutouts, I thought, *I'm never going to sleep.* So I started a new mental game. In my head, I began auctioning off tiny model cars online. The auctions only lasted seconds. I could barely keep up with the speed of my own thoughts. The cars sold for hundreds of thousands of dollars. Soon, strangers were joining in—listing more model cars, autographing them mid-auction, and watching the bids climb higher. I was the auctioneer, rattling off each price as the numbers flew past. I kept thinking, *This will never stop.* I told myself, *This has to be a dream.*

To test it, I opened my eyes and looked around. The hospital logo screensaver floated across the computer screen. I closed my eyes and opened them again—still there. I couldn't believe this was really happening.

Meanwhile, I was constantly grinding my teeth. They felt too big for my mouth. My jaw didn't feel lined up—side to side or front to back. I kept shifting it around, trying to make my teeth feel like they were in the right place.

I spent nearly a week without food, water, or medicine. Every day, I was told the same thing: I needed a feeding tube or I had to sign end-of-life papers. I refused. I didn't want to live with a tube sticking out of my belly. I didn't want to live that way. I was tired—tired of strokes, tired of fighting. I was ready to give up.

My mother visited almost every day, pleading with me to change my mind. But I had made my decision. I kept asking, *Why?* I kept praying to die. I felt angry every morning I woke up still alive. I was disgusted—miserable. All I wanted was peace.

On the sixth day, I was reminded again: feeding tube or end-of-life paperwork. This time, I told the doctor no without hesitation. I told him there was no point trying to survive—*I'll just keep having strokes.* I was proud of that decision. I couldn't wait to tell my mom.

Then I fell asleep. I had a dream. I don't remember what it was. I just know I had it. And when I woke up, everything was different. I was ready for the feeding tube.

I told the doctor, and they took me downstairs. My bed was rolled into a large room filled with hanging curtains. They closed the ones around me and put me to sleep. When I woke up, I had a clear tube coming out of my chest.

They took me back to my room. Then they moved me down a floor. I was finally excited—I was finally going to eat again. I was starving.

I fell asleep again. This time, I dreamed I was some kind of royal figure. I was on a private jet, on my way to meet my mother and tell her the good news: I had decided to get the feeding tube. On the flight, my servant was struggling to change my outfit. I wasn't helping—being paralyzed. She had to hold me up like I was a wet noodle as she tried to dress me.

I woke to find my diaper and hospital gown being changed. I had crashed hard. I'd been napping so well, I'd even started drooling. Then came my first "meal." Apparently, my brain was still recovering from the stroke, because I didn't realize I wouldn't actually be eating or tasting anything. For some reason, I was expecting a food tray. Instead, a nurse brought a clear plastic bottle of blended brown liquid. She turned it upside down, hung it on the IV pole, and set the timer on the feeding pump. The pump moved slowly and made a creaking sound as it pushed the liquid into my tube. It wasn't anything to be excited about. Still, I kept my eyes on it, just to make sure I was actually being fed. Afterward, the nurse poured some water into my feeding tube, but my throat still felt dry. Oddly enough, my favorite part of feeding time became watching that cup of water being poured. I stopped watching TV altogether—it drove me crazy seeing drinks being poured or advertised.

Once, I had a panic attack from muscle cramps. I couldn't move into a comfortable position. I was too weak to press the help button, and my voice barely worked. Still, I tried to get someone's attention. Some yells didn't even come out. Nurses told me to be quiet but never asked what I needed. I tried talking as they walked away. One turned off my lights and shut my door.

Later, a nurse came in to take my vitals. I was relieved to see him. I begged him for help. My head had slipped off the pillow, and my neck hurt badly. He clipped the oximeter to my finger, but I took it off—I was upset. He moved it to my toe. He recorded my vitals, ignoring my cries. He did finally adjust my head, but I had to beg him the whole time.

Another time, a nurse tried to give me medicine by mouth instead of through the tube. I resisted as he tried to open my mouth. Eventually, he gave up and used the feeding tube. That whole period was rough.

I felt ignored. Helpless. I couldn't speak clearly or press a button to call for help. I asked nurses to check on me regularly. Some did. Some didn't.

I remember getting sent downstairs for more MRIs. The transport guy set me in a special chair and rolled me down the hall. Along the way, I had muscle spasms and my head slipped off the headrest. I tried to get his attention, but he didn't stop. My neck became more and more uncomfortable. When we stopped at the elevator, I knew he heard me—he glanced down at me—but said nothing. I felt completely hopeless.

That's when I met Erin and Ariel.

Chapter 9 - Maybe There's a Chance

HEY, HEY, CHACE, WAKE UP. CHACE, WAKE
UP.

I wake to my dad gently shaking me. I'd been out
cold—like a baby.

"It's 9 o'clock. Time for dinner and meds."
Oh, great, I think to myself.

He grabs the remote and raises my bed. I can
already see the dinner tray waiting. It says "beef" on
the label, but I have my doubts. It's a pre-cooked,
pre-puréed mound of mystery. Smells like stink
bait. While I'm still groggy, he starts spoon-feeding
me. I feel Jack leap onto the bed. He probably
thinks I'm eating cat food. Be my guest, Jack.

Spoon after spoon, I'm counting down until it's
over. The food is awful, and honestly, I just want to
go back to sleep. Dad turns on the news—same
tired stories on repeat. I ask for a drink now and
then to help wash it down, but not often enough.
I've got this bad habit: I let the food sit and clog in
my throat. Sometimes, I can barely breathe.
Still, I don't panic. Not anymore. I just keep
swallowing and sucking in little gasps of air until
the next sip. But sometimes the clog gets worse
when I inhale. Then I glance at Dad and point my

middle finger at the cup. That means I need a drink. He's eyes are glued to the TV. I get an occasional bite.

I drift off, and my thoughts return to Nurse Erin and Ariel from the hospital.

They moved me again after discovering a leak— water on the floor from the sink. I'd have gladly licked it up if someone had helped me. My throat was that dry.

Nurse Erin and aide Ariel took over once I was in the new room. They were incredibly kind. They checked on me constantly and spent real time with me. I stayed with them for a few weeks. We talked a lot—it was therapy in itself. When I couldn't talk, Ariel would patiently write the alphabet on a dry-erase board and point to each letter while I spelled words with the slightest nod of my head.

I loved being around Ariel. She was beautiful— even with a face mask and her hair hidden under a cap. At one point, there was a miscommunication, and Ariel asked me if I was trying to ask her out. I told her I was in no position to do that—but admitted how much I wanted to. We kept talking about it. I loved those conversations. After that, Ariel became my reason to recover. I wanted to get better—for her.

By the end of my stay, my speech had improved. I was still slow, but mostly understandable. I could also move my right hand a little. When it came time to move again, I didn't want to leave—but I knew I had to. It was time for rehab. Ariel and I held hands and said goodbye—for now. Then they wheeled me down to the first floor.

"Last bite," my dad says. You have no idea how good it feels to hear that. "I'm through!" I say. Now I don't have to eat any more of that slop. Eat that! I imagine saying. He cleans up my tray and leaves the room.

The news is still showing the same recycled images. My head droops. Dad returns with my meds.

I swallow them quickly. He raises my cup to my lips, and I drink like I haven't had water in days. "Stay there and let your food settle," he says, walking out again. I couldn't go anywhere , even if the house were on fire. I'm so tired. I could fall asleep right here.

I'm thinking about Ariel—how sweet she was to me. I play a few games of checkers on my phone while memories of her run through my head. Then Dad comes back to change me and get me into bed.

When I moved down to the rehab floor, I could barely move my right hand. I wasn't expecting much results. I was in horrible shape, but wanted to get better for Ariel.

When in rehab, I saw several nurses, nursing aids, doctors, and therapists from the previous stroke. " Have you been here before?" and "You're back, what happened?" are two quotes that I remember hearing. My mom was visiting evenings. I had rehab nurses text Ariel for me on my phone, since I still couldn't move my fingers much.

I met many new faces as well. I became good friends with my nurse, Jenna. I was in rehab for twelve weeks. We spent a lot of time together. I became very attached to her.

In rehab, I had occupational therapy, physical therapy, and speech therapy on weekdays. Occupational therapy worked on my right arm and hand. Physical therapy worked on body positioning and my core. Speech therapy worked on my swallowing and talking. Jenna paid close attention to my improvements. She was happy to see what I accomplished.

I spent nearly every day with high hopes that Ariel would come visit after work. I watched the clock and practiced talking so she could understand me. She came by a couple of times. The text responses eventually stopped, and she stopped coming to see me.

In those twelve weeks, I achieved so much. I got a better attitude about being able to recover, and worked so hard. I gained some movement in my left arm and hand too. I gained enough strength in my core to hold myself up in the wheelchair with little help. I gained the strength to hold my head up again. I went from eating through a feeding tube to being able to eat pureed foods. The feeding tube was removed. I could finally drink thickened liquids. I can't explain how good that first gulp felt going down my throat and hydrating my dry insides. I went from hardly being able to get any words out to being able to speak sentences that people could understand.

Due to COVID-19, my dad wasn't allowed to visit until then. I was so happy to finally see him. He and my mother rotated visiting hours. I remember all the games I played and all the jokes I told in therapy. Some days were fun, and some were hard. I had someone come to dress me every morning. I got out of bed and in a wheelchair every day. I did my best to feed myself every meal. With a stand and a stylus, I even started texting on my phone again. Jenna and I texted every day.

The day came when it was time for me to leave the hospital. It was a very emotional day for me. Jenna showed up on her day off to say goodbye. I was rolled out on a stretcher while people stood in the hallway to wave bye. I was loaded up in an ambulance for a two-hour drive to a nursing facility. My dad met us there.

Either my dad or sister came to visit me at the facility nearly every day. There, I spent two more weeks. I went through all three therapies again. I enjoyed the speech therapy, but occupational and physical therapy left me in bed most days, and we didn't do much. I wasn't impressed at all. I wasn't happy there to say the least. One day, my friend Jenna came to see me. I was so surprised to see her. Another day, my brother-in-law's nieces and nephews showed up at the outside window. During COVID-19, the kids weren't allowed inside. It was so nice to finally get to see them, even though the glass.

The two weeks were over, and I finally got to go home. This time, I sat in my wheelchair and rode in the back of a van because it was only a ten-minute drive to my dad's new house that he recently purchased for us and his elderly parents. His efficiency apartment was too small for both of us, his parents, my cat, their cats, my wheelchair, and other equipment that I was going to need. We arrived at the new house, and I was unloaded and taken directly to my bed. I was still very weak and couldn't move my head around to see much of the house. Since then, we have found a caregiver to take care of me for a few hours during the day. We bought a patient lift and two manual wheelchairs. One for everyday use and one for the shower. He also, later on, bought me a power wheelchair.

In the next few weeks, my sister picked up my cat from my mother's house, and my mom sent me a TV for my new room. Mother also helped me sell my truck. My new life was very different and took months to adjust to.

Chapter 10 –Home

It's Sunday morning, and I've already been up
for five hours. Dad changed and fed me earlier.
Now, I'm sitting up in bed, waiting for him to take
me outside. He agreed after I asked, and I've been
looking forward to it. I can't wait to get out of this
bed. He should be back from cleaning up breakfast
any minute now—but he's been gone a while.

Finally, he walks into the room. "You good?" he
asks. I remind him I want to go outside.
"I have stuff I need to take care of first," he replies.
"You good?" he asks again.
I roll my eyes in disappointment. "Yeah," I
mumble. He leaves the room.

Hours pass. Then Dad comes in to finally take me
outside. He pets Jack for a moment—Jack's loving
it. But when Dad stops. Jack throws his paw out in
an attempt to snag Dad's hand.

Dad changes my diaper first, then slides the sling
underneath me. He uses the lift to hoist me up and
gently lowers me into my powered wheelchair. He
fastens the two safety belts, then takes hold of the
joystick. He doesn't let me drive inside.

At the front door, he hands me the controls. I ease
forward, guiding myself slowly down the threshold
ramp.

Once outside, I immediately turn up the speed. I like to go fast. It makes me feel less trapped in a boring wheelchair. Sometimes my eyes start scrolling up and down, and I have to slow down or stop. One trip from the cul-de-sac to the end of the short street and back at full speed is enough for me. I'm satisfied.

It's a beautiful day. The sun is bright and warm. It feels good to leave the house every now and then. I turn the speed down and drive up onto the sidewalk to meet my dad. We walk. I stop often to look at each house along the way. I get dizzy when I turn my head while driving.

We go up and down a few neighboring streets, then head back. I make occasional stops to reposition my grip on the joystick. It starts to slip after a few minutes, and I begin drifting to the side. I don't last long. I get tired quickly.

When we arrive home, I pause in the driveway, close my eyes, and soak in the sunlight while Dad opens his truck door and rummages around for something.

It's strange that I'm even here to enjoy this. A year and a half ago, I thought I was finished. I saw no way out. I was sure it was the end. I told the hospital staff that I didn't want to live anymore. I was done. I think about that sometimes—how I wanted to give up.

Now, I'm here. I'm getting by. I'm okay.

And I think about all the people who aren't here—people who took their own lives for far less. Perfectly healthy people who could walk, talk, and do everything they needed. No matter how hard it gets, don't be too quick to quit. Things change. Not always how we want, but still—they change. And sometimes, they get better.

It's a beautiful day, but I need to go back inside before I fall asleep in the driveway. I head up the slope toward the front door. Dad is already there. He opens the door as I drive up the ramp and into the house.

"Ready to get back in bed?" he asks.

I nod. I'm tired.

He takes over the joystick and steers me down the hallway to my room. He lifts me out of the chair and into bed with the lift. As he removes the sling from under me, he asks if I need to be changed again.

"Prolli," I say.

He checks. I passed. "Nope."

"You gonna nap?"

"Yas," I reply, more clearly this time.

He turns me on my right side and covers me with the sheet. Then he gives me the diver's 'OK' sign, asking for confirmation.

I nod.

He walks out and turns off the light.

Chapter 11- New Life

Rachel took very good care of me, but after years as my caregiver, she left due to personal reasons. Sara stepped in afterward, though she was only with me three mornings a week instead of five. Caregivers aren't cheap, and insurance didn't cover it, so we had to cut back.

Still, I made a commitment to fight through everything. I had to keep going. I believe it was my great-grandfather who once said, at a very old age, "You stop moving, you die."

I began recording and uploading videos of my efforts and dedication to becoming strong and independent again. I gained a small audience online, and their encouragement became incredibly important to me. My supporters—my word for them—inspired me to fight even harder.

Sara and I had so much fun making videos and exercising together. Despite everything I could no longer do, I was happy again. I had accepted what happened—four times now—and was finally moving forward. It was a new life, and a new beginning.

Sara and I stretched and exercised almost every day. After a year, I had come a long way. We accomplished so much, and I kept surprising myself with what I was able to do again. We used a ball. I still couldn't throw it, but my grip had improved. I had regained some movement in my right arm, though not enough to use it for much. What improved the most were my one-handed typing skills—with my right hand. My accuracy of using my stylus and my speed became much more reasonable.

On November 17, 2023, Sara came in and dressed me like any other day. She handed me my phone and left the room. I checked my social media and email. A few minutes later, she came back from the kitchen with my breakfast. I told her I wanted to film myself feeding myself. She set up the camera and started recording.

I started talking to the camera awkwardly, like I usually do. I don't remember what I was trying to say. After rambling a bit, I picked up my plastic fork with my right hand and tried to raise it to pick up my plastic fork. I immediately noticed I couldn't move my arm. That sometimes happens after my arm has been at rest for awhile. Usually, I can get it moving again by trying harder.

This time, I gave it everything I had. I even made some grunting noises, but nothing happened. At that point, I was really concerned. I let Sara know what was going on. I gave it one more hard pull, and my arm made it about halfway to my mouth before it started to fall back down quickly. I was also feeling a bit lightheaded. I was pretty sure I was having another stroke, but I wasn't thrilled—or ready—for another trip to the hospital.

I sat there thinking for a while. Out the window, I saw my dad mowing the lawn in the backyard. It was just bad timing—for both of us. I didn't want to ruin his day. But after a bit more thought, I finally told Sara to go outside and tell him I thought I was having another stroke. She left but came back shortly to say he couldn't hear her over the mower. I told her to get his attention and tell him we had an emergency. I was nervous to see his reaction. I felt like I had ruined everything.

But when dad came into the room, he didn't barge in or yell, like I had feared. He was calm and concerned. He asked me what was wrong and how I felt. After I explained, he asked if I thought I needed to go to the hospital. I nodded slowly, head down. He called 911, and we waited.

The ambulance arrived. The paramedics confirmed how I felt, took my vitals, and used my lift to get me out of bed and lower me onto a blanket on the floor. They folded it like a taco, each paramedic grabbing a piece, and carried me through the hallway and into the living room. They lowered me onto the stretcher, wheeled me outside, and loaded me into the ambulance. Sara jumped in and sat beside me on the bench, bringing an apple with her.

Moments later, the paramedic joined us, closed the door, and sat down beside Sara. As the ambulance pulled away, she grabbed supplies from the cabinets above and across from me. After getting what she needed, she sat back down. Then we heard a loud thump. She looked down and then at Sara, who had dropped her apple on the nasty floor and tried to pick it up. "Do not eat that!" the paramedic warned.

After sticking me with an IV, we arrived at the hospital. They rolled me into an exam room, and Sara followed. I hate going to the hospital because I can't explain to every doctor, nurse, and technician that I'm not a typical patient. I can barely hear, barely speak, and barely move. I was surprised when Sara stepped up and started talking to the staff on my behalf. She handled everything.

They gave me another IV and sent me for a brain MRI. When I returned, Sara was still there, but my dad had arrived and her shift was over. She left for another client, and dad and I waited several hours for the results. He made some phone calls while I played a word puzzle on my phone. I was relieved that I could use my right hand a little at that point. It was harder to move, but I expected it not to work at all. I used my left hand to guide and swing my right hand, but I could still get it to do what I needed.

Eventually, a doctor came in and shut the door behind him. He spoke to my dad for a while. Of course, I couldn't understand him, so I waited until he left and asked my dad what he said. dad told me the MRI showed a new stroke, and they wanted to keep me overnight.

I immediately shouted, as best I could, "NO, THEY CANNOT TAKE CARE OF ME HERE!" Dad knew what I meant. He tried to calm me down and explained it was a small stroke, and they only wanted to monitor me for two nights. I was upset—but not surprised.

Once in my room, Dad explained to the nurse that I could barely speak or hear and wasn't strong enough to press the call button. He asked them to check on me regularly. I rolled my eyes. I knew they wouldn't. I also knew it was close to shift change, and she'd be gone by 6 PM. I was way too familiar with hospitals.

Later, the kitchen brought a dinner tray, and Dad fed me. He said he had to work the next day but would return afterward. He told the staff to call him if they needed anything.

The next morning began with a phlebotomist waking me up and poking me with a needle. I call them vampires. My nurse actually showed up on time to feed me breakfast. The day dragged.

Some doctors came in to talk—without realizing I couldn't hear a word because no one had given me my hearing aid. I tried to ask them to call my dad, but I could barely get the words out. Eventually, most of them left and sent the nurse back in.

Lunch came, but no one came to feed me. The lunch lady took my untouched tray as if I had already eaten. She didn't realize the food was still there because of the dome-shaped cover over the plate. A short while later, my nurse came in and asked if I'd been fed. I nodded, disappointed. She apologized over and over, explaining that she had sent someone to help me eat. Neither I nor my stomach cared for the excuse. She brought me a sandwich and chips and fed me herself. As she did, she updated me on my test results and what was going on with my condition.

I stayed one more night in the hospital. I was so anxious to go home that I barely slept. The "vampire" came again that morning, and I let her poke me without protest—I was too tired to argue that they didn't need any more of my blood.

When I finally got to leave, it felt strange. My dad had to drive my powered wheelchair for me while I sat helplessly in the seat. Once home and in bed, I realized I couldn't reach the remote to adjust the bed or turn on the massager to ease the soreness from sitting so long. I missed having even that little bit of control.

Sara, my caregiver, came a few days later. I wasn't sure what we'd do—I felt like I couldn't do anything at all. I gave her my breakfast request:

pancakes, my favorite. She made them and fed me. It helped, just a little, to ease that feeling of defeat.

I don't remember much of what we did that day—it was just "baby stuff," basic things. The next two weeks were filled with simple therapy exercises, mainly focused on my hands. I couldn't do much, and the frustration was overwhelming.

Why couldn't the fourth stroke have been the last? I had already fought so hard. I had overcome so much. I had adapted. Still, Sara and I kept going, working on my arm and hand movement. I also got some therapy through insurance. And for the first time in a while, I felt like maybe everything was going to be okay. I had Sara by my side, helping me through it.

Chapter 12 -What do I have to work with

Here I was again—rehabilitating after a fifth stroke. I could barely move my arms and hands. I could no longer drive my wheelchair, use my bed remote, or do any of the exercises I had once practiced daily. Then, things took another devastating turn. It felt like the end of me for sure.

Sara and I had a brief conversation that left me stunned and deeply anxious about my future.

I felt broken and beaten—and Sara had been my only hope. So, when she told me she could no longer be my caregiver because she was expecting a baby, I didn't know what to do.

I immediately began trying to find a way to make things work. The physical strain of adjusting my body in bed or transferring me to a chair was simply too much for a pregnant woman. I realized there was no getting around it. And she was leaving at a time when I needed her most.

Thankfully, my new caregiver, Valerie, picked up her role quickly. We resumed work on my hands and fingers. Progress came—though slowly. It took immense patience.

My fingers were the biggest challenge. They clenched tightly into fists and refused to relax. It was extremely difficult for anyone to pry them open. We tried all sorts of methods to help—various gloves and finger splints—but nothing made it easy.

We practiced driving the wheelchair often. Being able to control it myself felt like the only independence I had left. It tore me apart that my arms could no longer extend properly, and my fingers refused to stay open. It wasn't just about driving the chair. I used to be able to press every button—adjust the speed, tilt the chair back to lie down. That was freedom to me.

We tried arm braces and bungee cords to keep my driving arm straight. But nothing worked perfectly. We played simple games and did regular exercises. They were frustratingly difficult—my fingers always seemed to get in the way.

I used a stationary hand cycle to stretch and move my arms. It was a good form of exercise. I wore special gloves that wrapped around my hands to keep them secured to the pedals. Some days, I reached my rotation goals easily. Other days were brutally hard. Sometimes I couldn't even finish because I was too tired or my arm muscles were too stiff. On those days, we stopped at a low number and tried again the next day.

Valarie was my caregiver for a year before she, too, had to leave and was replaced.

There's no doubt I worked hard. No doubt I gave everything I had—again and again. I've been hospitalized five times due to strokes. If you count the brain tumor, I've fallen six times and kept going.

1) Brain tumor in 1991
2) Stroke in 2016
3) Stroke in 2018
4) Stroke in 2019
5) Stroke in 2020
6) Stroke in 2023

I owe everything to my family. I couldn't have done any of this without them—especially my dad. He has been there for me from day one. He gave up so much to care for me. Instead of living out the life he imagined, he has dedicated himself to mine— finding caregivers so he can go to work, or spending entire weekends taking care of me himself.

Sometimes I get depressed thinking about what could have been. If life hadn't pushed me into the gutter, I'd still be working. I'd still be living. I might have married. I might have had a son. I'd still be walking, still talking, still doing so much more.

It hurts knowing how much I've missed out on. It's been so long since I could dress myself, brush my hair, drive a car, or do the countless little things people take for granted. Now I'm stuck in bed.

I spent years in school. And now, it feels like it was for nothing. Sometimes I wonder: what if I could go back and finish my architecture degree? Maybe it would be more fun this time around. On the other hand, I say I wish I had never stepped foot on that campus at all. I feel like I wasted all that time without earning a degree. And when I'm feeling bitter, I think: if I'd known I would end up like this, I never would've gone to college at all.

I guess I have regrets. A lot of them. I wish I had danced more. Smiled more. I wish I had made more of an effort to meet people, to make friends. I wish I had dated more, enjoyed life more. I wish I had taken life a little less seriously. Then again, how could I have known it would come to this.

I remember being told about the least fortunate brain tumor survivors when I had mine removed. I was told—many times—how lucky I was. Maybe this was how I was meant to be all along. Maybe life just had to catch up with me.

Now, I sit here watching everyone else as their lives unfold like perfect, enjoyable fairytales. Sometimes I just want to call time-out. This isn't how things are supposed to go. This is extremely unfair! How do I reset my life? Surely, this must be a system glitch.

I don't actually mind being in a wheelchair. What really gets me is not being able to talk well, my hearing, the use of my arms, and my core strength. I fall over like a sack of potatoes because I can't sit upright for long. I can't even use my arms to hold myself up—they're just too weak.

Some days, staying positive feels impossible. I get very lonely when my caregiver isn't around, and I often feel discouraged. People are busy, and I feel like I just cause more problems. I usually stay in bed with the door closed. I keep my cat in, and my ceiling fan runs all day—otherwise, I wake up drenched in sweat.

Most of my day is spent browsing the internet, reading the news on my phone, or playing a few games. Then I'll watch TV with captions. I'm not fast enough to read all the words, but I still enjoy watching, even if I ignore the text. I love watching baseball games.

I have some apps and tools that help me through the daily challenges. Two apps can speak for me when I can't. One of them even transcribes speech when I can't hear well. It works on videos, too—even when my phone is muted.

I try not to press the call button unless I absolutely have to. People get annoyed, especially when they're busy—and they're almost always busy. It's also a struggle just to push the button. I often can't reach the call button that is on a band around my left wrist. I have to reach for the one around my neck. At times, even when I have the button in my hand, I can't press it. My fingers go limp and can't apply pressure. Sometimes I can't reach either button at all, and my only hope is to call out for help. But often, my voice is too faint to be heard.

I can't scratch my nose or my head when they itch—and they itch a lot. I struggle with almost every task. I still choke on food. I've turned blue and nearly died at least four times. I have a suction device for those emergencies. So far, I've been lucky. My dad has only had to use it like, maybe... a lot.

Life isn't always a fairytale—but we have to keep going. Life is a beautiful gift, even when we don't understand why it is the way it is. People have struggled since the beginning of time. You just have to keep moving—because life goes on, with or without you.

Don't give up. Don't let death win. Keep fighting until the end. Keep fighting!

I don't know when the next stroke will come. I don't know if it will kill me, put me in a coma, or leave me unable to communicate. I don't know if it'll even come at all. All I know is that tomorrow is another day—and I have to keep moving.

That is my story.
This is my fight.
This is my revival.